PRAY IT AGAIN, SAM

Imprimatur:
Monsignor Edward J. O'Donnell
Vicar General, Archdiocese of St. Louis

Our Sunday Visitor Publishing Division
Our Sunday Visitor, Inc.
200 Noll Plaza
Huntington, Indiana 46750

International Standard Book Number:
0-87973-461-2
Library of Congress Catalog Number:
91-61272

Cover design by Rebecca J. Heaston

Printed in the United States of America

461

PRAY IT AGAIN, SAM

Reverend Kenneth J. Roberts

Our Sunday Visitor Publishing Division
Our Sunday Visitor, Inc.
Huntington, Indiana 46750

TABLE OF CONTENTS

INTRODUCTION

When was the last time God spoke to you? I love that question. You wouldn't believe some of the answers I receive. I think I'm mostly amused by the reactions of the people whom I am addressing. I can usually tell by the expressions on their faces what they're thinking. Some discreetly nudge their neighbor and roll their eyes as if to say, "This guy is a nut." Others stare back at me as if to ask, "Does God speak to YOU?" When I really want to shake them, I say, "He speaks to me every day." But rather than risk being shepherded away from the pulpit, I always hasten to add, "At Mass!" Then, I go on to qualify the other ways God speaks to us, through Scripture, thoughts, feelings, and people.

Once when I was directing a retreat to a group of women, I asked that question: WHEN WAS THE LAST TIME GOD SPOKE TO YOU? I peered at my retreatants, employing enough dramatics to provoke shock and grab their attention. Suddenly a woman jumped from her chair and proudly proclaimed, "God talked to me two years ago, while I was making a novena to the Sacred Heart of Jesus!" This time the dumbfounded look was on my face. I was totally off guard as I found myself stammering for the right words, but what do you say to someone to whom God has spoken? And I mean REALLY spoken, or at least that's how it was indicated by the very firm, matter-of-fact tone in her response.

Since that time, I have learned to fortify myself with a number of ways to get the ball back when someone catches me off guard like that.

My whole point in asking when God last spoke to you is to illustrate that we don't listen enough at prayer, whether it's during the Scripture readings at Mass or alone. The fact is, GOD DOES SPEAK TO YOU and in many ways, but you're never going to hear Him if you're not listening.

Do you remember the Old Testament reading from 1 Samuel, chapter 3, verses 1-18? "Speak, Lord, your servant is listening." Well, before Samuel got around to the "listening" part, God had called him three times, but he didn't answer. He was sleeping, and the best part . . . "in the temple." Maybe he fell asleep because he ran out of things to say . . . or shall I say, "pray"? That's very true of many of us in our prayer life. We present ourselves to God, armed with all our prayers, all the things we want to say to Him. Maybe it's a petition, or an expression of gratitude, or a favorite psalm of praise. Whatever we plan on telling God, we run out of what we have to say, then we get up and leave, never waiting to hear what He has to say to us. We're doing all the talking.

In Samuel's case, he went to sleep. The Lord called him three times, but Samuel didn't know it was the Lord. Perhaps we don't always recognize when He is speaking to us also. Finally, after Eli advised Samuel that it was the Lord, he responded with, "Speak, Lord, your servant is LISTENING."

Prayer is listening too. Defined in the dictionary, prayer is a "communion with a deity," and to have communion there has to be more than just one. Communion is communication, and how often have we heard that communication is broken when only one person does all the talking? That's true in all areas of communication — business, family life, and even prayer.

Often when counseling during retreats, I hear, "Father, I just can't pray," or "I try to pray, but it just doesn't come out right," or "I don't feel as if God hears my prayer." I guarantee you, He does. You just haven't listened for the answer, or perhaps recognized the answer. I suppose the most tremendous thing I can share with you is the fact that GOD HEARS YOU! Don't worry about it. He knows all about you, what your needs are, and what your desires are. . . . He's very much aware, but often *we* get them confused.

In this book, I want to offer you some explanation about the various forms of prayer, some old and some new, and hopefully you will find some aids to incorporate in your own prayer life, or at least, perhaps, you will better understand others in their ways of praying. Many people are confused by some of our present liturgies, but I feel that often it is because they have not been educated about them. Also, I find in many cases that there is intolerance and a judgmental attitude if some choose to pray differently from the way we do. That is truly unfortunate; no one has the right to judge another's prayer simply because he or she does not understand it.

I have divided this book into four parts. In Part One, the first three chapters, the focus is on liturgical prayer, and as we are Catholics, the center of our prayer life is the liturgy of the Mass. I hope you will gain a deeper appreciation and understanding of the Holy Sacrifice by offering you ways to participate more fully at each liturgy.

Part Two stresses the need for private prayer, and the need to develop a personal relationship with God. Hopefully, you will examine where He fits in your life, then resolve to let Him work more fully by seeking ways to draw closer to Him.

Part Three examines various forms of prayer. Perhaps you will find one that will enable you to grow in your spiritual life and deepen your communication with Our Lord.

In the last section of this book, Part Four, I have offered a few meditations that may help you to develop your thoughts and imagination in prayer.

If I may say it at this point, I don't have all the answers. I'm trying to get to heaven just like you, and what you read is information I have gathered from study, but also from very holy people who have shared their Christ experience with me.

There is one thing of which I am certain . . . we all need to pray and communicate with our God in our own personal way.

God wants YOUR prayer. He wants the praise that YOU alone can offer Him. He has something important to say to you too. Samuel had to be called three times before he answered with the "prayer of listening." You might say that he had to be told: PRAY IT AGAIN, SAM.

PART ONE

Liturgical Prayer

1

'It Used to Be Such a Nice Church'

This is definitely one of my favorite stories:

An elderly priest attended a somewhat lively liturgy in another parish. Huge banners in brilliant colors were hanging from every available spot. The music was extremely loud, with trumpets, guitars, drums, and tambourine keeping a fast beat. Liturgical dancers, all wrapped up in long white flowing robes, accompanied the main celebrant in the entrance procession, while a few of the congregation clapped their hands in rhythm with the tempo.

The young priest who accompanied the old priest was very much aware of his elder's traditional preference, so he kept looking at him throughout the Mass to study his reaction. But there was no reaction. The old cleric simply kept his eyes fixed on the altar, and only occasionally did he glance down at his open missalette. His face was expressionless.

When the liturgy ended, everyone filed out of the church in a very joyful mood, smiling at one another, hugging one another, and "praising the Lord" in more than audible voices. The old priest seemed oblivious to all that was happening around him. No comment. No expression. Finally, the young priest couldn't stand it any longer. "How did you like the liturgy, Monsignor?" he asked.

The old priest paused for a few seconds, looked blankly back at him, and in a very defeated tone, answered, "It used to be such a nice church!"

True, this story is humorous, but there's a quiet sadness about it also. People confide in me all the time that they are confused by some contemporary liturgies. Some even feel that the Church has deserted them along with all they held dear and sacred for many years. They are not comfortable with the "new" ways, and that is probably because they have never had the changes in liturgy completely explained to them.

I remember one lady telling me about the time she was on vacation and found the local

Catholic church so she could attend her Sunday-obligation Mass. It so happened that it was on a Saturday evening, and a charismatic liturgy was scheduled. She had never attended one before so she was quite overwhelmed after a few people began praising "in tongues."

The hum gradually filled the church. Totally confused by it all, she tapped the stranger's shoulder beside her and asked, "Excuse me. I'm traveling and not familiar with the area . . . am I in a CATHOLIC church?"

She was assured that, indeed, she was in a CATHOLIC church, but she said that was even more bewildering. "l don't understand all of this, Father. What's happening to our Church? All that carrying on . . . I could hardly say my prayers!"

It's sometimes difficult to explain that what she referred to as "all that carrying on" is prayer, but that it's just not the form of prayer familiar to her. Still, it is no more — or no less — sincere than her kind of prayer.

Please understand, at this point I am not trying to convince you to pray that way . . . that's a personal choice. Rather, I am only trying to help you better understand others' ways of praying and hopefully discourage the tendency we all have to judge others' sincerity by the way they pray.

I often use the following analogy. Some plants require lots of water and light to flourish, while others require shade and less water. If you tried to put them in the wrong place, they might very well die. You can't force a plant to grow if you don't provide the elements to which it is best suited.

Think of the Church as a gardener who knows how to look after his plants. He is aware that each type of plant has different needs, so in order to have a beautiful garden where his plants can grow and flourish, he provides what each must have. Likewise, Holy Mother Church wants her children to grow in their spiritual lives, so she offers us many different means, knowing that each of us has different needs. But, she doesn't *force* us to aspire to one way of prayer. She offers several from which we can choose the best one for us.

Hopefully, you are in a parish that provides both traditional and modern liturgies, but if you find yourself in a situation that causes you confusion, don't worry. And don't get hung up about the things that aren't essential. Concentrate on what *is* essential, and I'm certain you know that at Mass the Scripture readings and the Eucharist are the essentials. The Mass is still the Mass . . . and Jesus is truly present in the Eucharist. That has not changed. Whether you approach the Precious Body and Blood accompanied by bongo drums or Gregorian chant, Jesus is waiting for *you*.

What a beautiful gift! Jesus Christ gives Himself to us. The music, the vestments, the banners — they are all just the wrappings, but the Church in her wisdom knows that the packaging must have appeal. If you purchased a priceless gem for someone, wouldn't you buy the gift wrap and ribbon for the bow that would most appeal to that individual? Would you buy wrapping paper depicting teddy bears and toys for an adult? Would you choose a floral pattern for a football player?

Our Church is striving to provide appeal through music, songs, banners, etc., to many people and many age-groups, and although it may appeal to some, others may be turned off. Hopefully, the presence of Christ in the Eucharist still remains the center of it all.

Even the "handshake of peace" is difficult for some, and they can't understand why it has become a part of the liturgy of the Mass. "Father, I feel stupid shaking hands with someone I don't even know." I often wonder if any of us would recognize Jesus if He were next to us. He did say, "Whatever you do to the least of my brothers, that you do unto Me." Would any of us refuse to take the hand of Jesus? If you have difficulty in the handshake of peace, or if it is not totally comfortable for you, try to understand that Our Lord is in that person beside you. We are made in the "image and likeness of God."

Don't isolate the Risen Christ by locking Him up in the tabernacle. There, He is physically present in the Blessed Sacrament, but His Spirit is within all of us, you and me . . . and that includes that stranger on your right or left at Mass.

It often amuses me when I gaze on the faces of the congregation and a few have that pained look. You know, I can't help but feel that many have kept an old expression foremost in their spiritual lives . . . *prayer and suffering*. But here's the good news . . . it's *prayer and joy*! We can acquire both peace and joy through prayer. What can give us more joy than to know that we have the Bread of Eternal Life? But I doubt if all of us really fathom what that means, or it seems to me that if we did, we couldn't help but feel joy, and non-essentials would not trouble us so much.

If you are one of those people who prefer very lively liturgies, perhaps you feel quite pleased with yourself by what you have just read. Well, hold on a second . . . I have something to say to you too. Don't upstage the Lord!

The Mass is not only a celebration, it is a sacrifice. It *IS* the Sacrifice of the Mass and we proclaim this in our acclamation of faith: "Christ has died. Christ has risen. Christ will come again."

Christ *suffered* and died, and that should provoke a response within each of us, because although Christ has risen and will come again is reason to be joyful, reverence for the Sacrifice at Calvary must not be overlooked.

As I have stated earlier, the liturgy should

23

be appealing, but let's not confuse that with "entertaining." Don't become so wrapped up in staging the liturgy of the Mass that emphasis shifts from the Eucharistic Banquet and becomes the Eucharistic Buffet . . . that Jesus Christ's presence in the Blessed Sacrament is just sandwiched in somewhere between the entrance procession, the music, the hugging, and in some instances, the dance. I doubt if the Last Supper had choreography, but I doubt if there was a choir and Gregorian chant either. Focus in on what is essential, the Liturgy of the Word and the Liturgy of the Eucharist. It's all a matter of personal choice, and at the risk of sounding redundant, I feel compelled to repeat: "Music and various forms of liturgy are not the essentials . . . they're just the wrappings. The Church has *not* changed her teaching that Jesus Christ is present under the appearance of bread and wine."

If you feel the Church has changed too fast and deserted you, be assured that she has not. We still say the same Apostles' Creed. We still say the same Lord's Prayer (and Hail Mary). We still have the same sacraments. We still hold the same teachings of the

Church to be true. Methods have been altered somewhat to adapt to a changing world . . . the essentials are still the same.

Perhaps you feel the changes are not going fast enough; be patient. Wait for the Holy Spirit to help us catch up.

Be assured, any of you who have doubts about our Catholic Faith . . . IT STILL IS A NICE CHURCH!

PRACTICAL APPLICATION

1. Think back over the Masses you attended in the last year. How many disturbed you? How many comforted you?

2. Why were you disturbed or comforted?

3. Was it *essential* to the Mass?

4. After Mass, did you make any resolutions to live by and practice throughout the week?

5. How much time did you spend alone with Christ after you received Holy Communion?

PRAY IT AGAIN, SAM

2

Get a Word 'Out'

ESSENTIALS, that's where we must direct our priorities; moreover, our faith. As we are Catholic Christians, the Mass must be the center of our prayer life, and it is "essential" that we understand the dynamic phenomenon that occurs each time we attend the Eucharistic Feast. GOD SPEAKS TO US! And Christ is present in two ways, the Liturgy of the Word and the Liturgy of the Eucharist.

In the Liturgy of the Word, the Scripture readings, He speaks directly to us. So what did He say to you last Sunday at Mass? Do you remember what Scriptures were read in the first and second readings and in the Gospel? There was something there that God wanted you alone to hear . . . do you remember?

Just as in the story of Samuel, when God called to him three times, so did He speak to you three times . . . and what did He say? If you can't remember, don't feel too bad, because unfortunately, you are in the majority. Still, if I were to ask you what you had for breakfast last Sunday before or after Mass, could you answer? It seems we are all pretty attentive to what nourishment we put into our bodies, but too often we neglect the nourishment we need for our souls. And in some instances, we are suffering from spiritual malnutrition.

Admittedly, it is sometimes difficult to digest all the readings and apply them to our lives, especially since we often find that all the readings do not relate to one another, or they don't match up. Perhaps this story will give you some insight and help you in your personal application of the readings you hear at Mass.

A nun friend of mine was being transferred to a different mission. She was a delightful, bubbly woman who enjoyed life and made the most out of every occasion. I planned a small dinner party at a very fine restaurant as a farewell-appreciation celebration. Sister was almost childlike as she examined the delicate crystal and elaborate place settings. Then came the menu.

As in many gourmet restaurants, the

menu was quite discriminating, offering only a few choice appetizers, a few select entrées of meat, fish, or fowl, and of course a few beautiful, lavish desserts. Since Sister was not able to translate the French menu, she asked the waiter for assistance. He was more than helpful as he proceeded to describe each item on the menu.

The expression on Sister's face puzzled me . . . she seemed almost dumbfounded. Finally, when the waiter completed his almost poetic explanation of the last item on the menu, he waited for her response. Holding her index finger in the air, she nodded and made a "just one minute" sort of gesture, then leaned toward me and in an audible, apologetic whisper, she pleaded, "Father, I can't possibly eat *ALL of that*!"

Our small dinner party broke up laughing as Sister's face reddened. She knew her statement was the cause of the reaction, but she wasn't certain just why. After assuring her that in no way was she expected to eat "all of that," I directed her to choose which dish was most appealing to her. She made a relieved sigh, then proceeded to order the dish she preferred from the many that were offered.

Whenever I am trying to teach retreatants, teens, or whomever I address about how to get the most out of the Liturgy of the Word, I give them the same direction that I gave Sister, "Choose a word or a phrase that appeals to you." You are not expected to digest all of what you hear. Some people may be able to accomplish that, but for those of us who cannot, picking one word or phrase works best.

I guarantee you, if you pay attention and *listen* to the readings, really listen, one word or phrase will hit you. Get that word *out*, think about it, apply it to your life or a situation you are presently trying to deal with. Get the word out. Listen to what God is saying to you. It's your word, so take it with you when you leave Mass and during those quiet moments throughout the day or week, think about that word. GOD HAS SPOKEN TO YOU.

I really believe that if you attend each Mass with the intention of getting spiritual nourishment for your soul, and you really listen to what God is saying to you in the

Scripture readings, you will not be distracted by the nonessentials.

When I'm discussing the Mass as the center of our prayer life with teens, one of the common complaints is "The Mass is boring." But I don't just hear that from teens, I hear it from our more mature Catholics as well. And my answer is the same to whatever age-group I am addressing: "The Mass is boring only if you don't understand it, or you don't fully participate."

There are some who complain, "I don't get anything out of the Mass . . . it's the same old thing." My response to this is that you will never get anything out if you don't put something in!

So, we have two problems concerning boredom at Mass: lack of understanding of the liturgy, and non-participation. Perhaps I can illustrate this more effectively by sharing an incident that happened to me when I first came to the United States.

I was born and raised in England and studied for the priesthood in Rome, so like all Europeans, my favorite sport is soccer. That's a sport I can really get involved in and cheer along with the most enthusiastic fans.

But when I first came to the United States, I found myself assigned to a Dallas parish where every Sunday afternoon was spent glued to the television and it was my luck to arrive at the start of the football season. Everybody in the parish, including the pastor and his assistants, was a fanatic about the Dallas Cowboys, and this was evident from the way the church parking lot drained in record time after the last Sunday Mass. You could bet that everyone was heading either for the stadium or a television set. In my rectory, everyone was paralyzed before the tube, and I learned quickly that first Sunday game that I dare not try to converse or, God forbid, ask a question during the game because I was SSSSHHHHHed immediately. Not only did they shackle themselves before the set on Sunday, they discussed the game, play by play, at mealtime during the week. I was certain that everyone was suffering from the same obsession, FOOTBALL, Dallas Cowboys Football.

So rather than compete with the kickoff or announcer, or the groans when they felt a bad play had been called, or the cheers when they made a first down, I quietly took my assigned seating place in the recreation room and predisposed myself mentally to a boring few hours. How I hated those first few Sunday afternoons in Texas. There I sat, a hushed child, watching three men (priests, at that) jump up and cheer, or slump and pout in their seats if somebody did something wrong on the screen. And desperation . . . God knows, few more desperate looks have ever appeared on human faces to compare with those worn by my colleagues when the score was tied and Dallas needed to get the ball back in time to score.

Once after a victory and what all the priests referred to as a "fantastic game," one of the priests slapped me on the back and in a jubilant tone, asked, "What do you think of our American football now, Ken?" (As if winning would have made a difference to my ignorance and dislike of the game.)

I answered honestly, "To tell you the truth, Monsignor, I think football is boring." He could not have been more shocked if I had voiced heresy. He looked at me almost as if he had pity for me. Gathering all the patience he could muster, he tried a new approach. "The only reason you find it boring is because you don't understand the game and you can't get excited at what's going on."

I admitted that he was probably right and I offered to learn something about this Sunday obsession if he had the patience to teach me. That was sixteen years ago. Now I cheer, jump up, shout, and wave my hands in the air just like the rest of the fans. (But I do this for the Phoenix [formerly St. Louis] Cardinals . . . I've been out of Texas for more than twenty years.)

When I had told the priest that I thought the game was boring, I wasn't telling him a thing about the game; I was telling him something about myself. It was boring because I didn't understand it and I wasn't putting anything into it.

I respond the same way to people who complain that the Mass is boring and they don't get anything out of it. I tell them, "You are not telling me a thing about the Mass, but you're telling me a lot about you." Perhaps many of you have not learned to "play the game" at Mass.

The Mass is divided into two parts, the Liturgy of the Word and the Liturgy of the

Eucharist. At the Liturgy of the Word, Scripture is read to you three times plus in the Responsorial Psalm. Your responsibility is to *get a word out*.

Remember my story about the nun in the restaurant? Well, think of the Scripture readings at Mass as a menu. You can't digest and absorb all that is offered, so choose that word or phrase that is most appealing to you or that mostly applies to your particular situation, then *feed on it*. God is speaking to YOU. It's really amazing how many people will hear the same readings and when I ask them what word or phrase they chose, each will be different. Occasionally a few may pick the same, but their interpretation will be different, and the application will differ from one individual to another. So, it's safe to assume that whatever word you took out, that's the one God meant for you. It's YOUR word, your phrase, your line, yours to feed on and to apply to your life and grow closer to the Lord.

God spoke to you last Sunday . . . what did He say?

PRACTICAL APPLICATION

1. Do you remember any of the readings from last Sunday's Scriptures?

2. Did you apply anything you heard at Mass last Sunday to your everyday routine during the week?

3. If you find Mass boring, have you honestly done anything to make it more exciting and meaningful for you?

4. At your next Mass, get a word OUT, then "feed on it."

PRAY IT AGAIN, SAM

3

Get a Word 'In'

Just as I told you to get a word "out" at the Liturgy of the Word at Mass, so I am directing you to put a word "in" at the Liturgy of the Eucharist. That word is "amen."

Even in secular terms, the word "amen" is used as an expression of agreement or affirmation, but most Christians tag it on the end of almost every prayer, i.e.,

. . . world without end, AMEN.

. . . now and at the hour of our death, AMEN.

. . . but deliver us from evil, AMEN.

. . . life everlasting, AMEN.

. . . for yours is the kingdom, the power, and the glory, forever and ever, AMEN.

. . . rest in peace, AMEN.

. . . to amend my life, AMEN.

Do you recognize the endings of familiar prayers that we as Catholics say frequently? It seems that we have become so accustomed to mumbling "amen" at the end of every prayer, and we do it so automatically, that we never really fathom what it means. Try to concentrate on the fact that saying the word "amen" is your signature of agreement or affirmation. We are saying "yes" to the prayer we have just recited, and we are acknowledging our belief and faith in those words. So the next time you pray and tag that "amen" on the end, go over the prayer and really examine what you have just proclaimed to believe.

In this chapter, I hope to make the Mass come more alive to you by explaining the "Great Amen" we say during the Liturgy of the Eucharist. Keep in mind that the Eucharistic sacrifice is the people of God coming together to reenact the renewal of the covenant made by Jesus Christ on our behalf. The covenant is the solemn agreement, or contract, that Jesus made in His death and in His resurrection to redeem us and offer us eternal life with the Father.

The priest as the presider of the Liturgy pronounces God's holy AMEN. The "amen" that causes something to be. When God says, "AMEN" . . . it is!

During the Mass, the priest speaks for

Christ, "This is My Body . . . this is My Blood." At that moment, the bread and wine become the Body and Blood of Jesus Christ. He has said His "amen."

St. Paul tells us in First Corinthians, "Is not the bread we bless the Body of Christ? Is not the cup we bless the Blood of Christ?" From the Last Supper to this present day, whether it's recited in Latin, Greek, Hebrew, or English, it is the same thing. Whether it is recited to the background of Gregorian chant, organ music, the Sistine choir, guitars, or bongo drums, it is still the same thing. "CHRIST HAS DIED, CHRIST HAS RISEN. CHRIST WILL COME AGAIN". . . and again and again.

The Eucharistic prayer said by the priest begins with the preface as he invites us to "lift up your hearts." You respond, "We have lifted them up to the Lord." Now you are ready to give thanks and praise to the Father through Jesus' name in the Spirit. The prayer concludes, "Through Him, with Him, in Him, in the unity of the Holy Spirit, all honor and glory is Yours, Almighty Father, forever and ever. . ."

Now is the time for the most important

word ever to be uttered by you. Now you are invited to put your signature to the covenant, or contract, already signed by the Blood of Christ. He has said "amen" to you, and now He awaits your "amen" to Him. He has already said, "amen" to His giving Himself to you, and now He awaits the "amen" for your giving yourself to Him.

When God says, "amen," we surrender to His will. For us, "amen" has many meanings . . . let it be, yes, I surrender, I give in, I believe.

Recall the last Mass you attended. The priest held up the chalice and host. God's AMEN was completed, and the bread and wine became the Body and Blood of Christ. How did you respond to this miracle?

Ideally, the congregation should gaze at the altar and, with eyes of faith, shout, "Amen" . . . the great AMEN. Is that what really happens to you? Do you attend Mass with that kind of faith? Always? At every Mass? Perhaps a few words of encouragement may help here.

A young boy was brought to me a few years ago because he had been refused First Communion by his pastor since he had told the pastor that he didn't believe the bread and wine was really the Body and Blood of Christ.

I questioned the young boy, who had an unusually high intelligence, why he didn't believe in the real presence of Christ in the Eucharist. He answered that since it looked like bread and tasted like bread, and since it looked like wine and tasted like wine, it must be bread and wine. I asked him, "What if I took the bread and wine and exposed it to radiation . . . would you eat and drink it?" His answer was a quick and certain, "No!"

"Why not?" I asked.

"Because it would be radioactive."

"But it would still look like bread and wine and it would still taste like bread and wine," I argued.

"Yeah, but something would have happened to it."

He and I both agreed on that. Something would have happened to the bread and wine that could not be sensed, and if we were to eat that bread and wine, we would be eating radiation . . . under the APPEARANCE of bread and wine.

You and I have to say "amen" to science

on that one . . . so why not say "amen" to God then when the priest repeats Christ's words, "This is My Body . . . This is My Blood." I met that same young man coming out of Mass ten years later. He reminded me of our earlier conversation, a conversation that changed his life. Since his first Communion, he has almost always gone to daily Mass, because, as he put it, "Now that I believe that it really is Jesus, I can't wait until the next Sunday to get it."

He says his "amen" almost every day. How about you? Isn't it hard to stay away from the Eucharist knowing that it is the REAL THING?

AMEN is the greatest prayer we can say. We are never too tired, too sick, too hungry, too poor, too young or too old to utter it. Get used to praying it at Mass to the greatest prayer that Christ ever prayed for us. When the priest says, "Through Him, with Him, in Him, in the unity of the Holy Spirit, all honor and glory is Yours, Almighty Father, forever and ever. . ." shout it out. Always get that word IN. "AMEN."

I guarantee the Mass will come alive for you as you become more alive in Christ!

PRACTICAL APPLICATIONS

1. When you say the Lord's Prayer and you say "amen" at the end, you have just put your signature on the words of that prayer. Do you *really* mean "Thy will be done"?

2. Also, in the Lord's Prayer, have you really forgiven those who "trespassed" against you?

3. At Mass, have you surrendered yourself to God as you claim in the GREAT AMEN?

4. The next time you say some of your favorite prayers, really *think* about what you are saying and what is required of you when you "sign your covenant" by saying "amen."

PRAY IT AGAIN, SAM

PART TWO

The Need
for Prayer

4

'Why Me, God?'

Haven't you said *that* one time or another in your life when things didn't go as you planned or the way that you prayed they would?

Maybe you were misjudged or treated unfairly by someone whom you loved and respected. Maybe you lost your job or had an accident when your automobile insurance had just run out. Maybe you experienced one trial after another and you felt you didn't deserve all these tribulations, then in desperation, you cried out, "Why me, God?"

Some people rebel and turn away from God, because they feel their prayers have been unheard and God doesn't care. But are trials and sufferings any easier to bear without Him? NEVER!

I went to a close friend and asked her permission to tell this story.

A few years ago, she was hospitalized for severe depression. Those of us who knew her well were shocked, because she had always projected a cheerful personality and she had a way of giving comfort to others when they were down, assuring them that God looks after everything "so don't give up hope." Her message was always, "Trust God . . . Father knows best."

She went to Mass almost daily and she was sensitive to others' problems, so appropriately she was the one to whom so many friends turned for support and consolation. Because of this, I was numb when I learned that she had deliberately overdosed and was in an intensive-care unit. From there she was transferred to a psychiatric hospital for observation and, hopefully, rehabilitation.

On the way to visit her, I found myself probing for the right words to share with her, and no matter what I came up with in my mind, I felt they would be ineffective because she had probably used the same words herself when comforting others, but obviously they no longer held any meaning for her, or she would not be in this state. I prayed hard as they unlocked the door to the ward where she had been assigned.

For the first fifteen minutes of our

meeting, the conversation was awkward and strained as we exchanged dialogue about the bad weather, the tastefully decorated hospital parlor, my retreat schedule, and so on. Her voice was shallow and indifferent. Finally, after saying a silent prayer, I reached for her hand. "I know this is all very painful for you, but trust God to. . ."

"Trust God!" she interrupted with a shout. "Don't talk to me about trusting God. For twenty years I have prayed and begged God to make my marriage right . . . and during those twenty years, I have been through a lot, but I really trusted God would pull it all together. Then, just when I thought all my prayers were answered, that my marriage and family were at peace, my husband tells me he wants a divorce. Everything I have worked for, prayed for, and trusted God to make happen is gone. I DID TRUST God and where did it get me?"

Her anger gave way to tears, and I felt helpless to offer her any consolation. When I left her, I promised to pray for her, but she almost seemed to resent my offer. She had cut God out of her life, but she still had pain.

I was on a retreat schedule that took me

out of town for a couple of weeks, but during that time I kept my promise; I did pray for her and I asked many others to pray for my special intention also. As soon as I got back in town I went to see her, but I felt some anxiety as I wondered if her attitude had changed at all. I was almost afraid she would be bitter with me because she seemed to resent my offer of prayer so deeply.

The nurse told me that my friend was in the chapel and that Mass was probably just finishing, so I decided to meet her there. I was relieved to know that she had turned back to God, and I was anxious to learn what had happened to get her back.

When I entered the chapel I found my friend kneeling alone in the last pew. The priest had just finished distributing Holy Communion as I knelt beside her. I could tell she was more at peace when she looked up at me, smiled, and squeezed my hand. "I'm glad you're here, Father Ken," she whispered.

"And I'm glad you're *here*!" I answered. She smiled knowingly. As the priest was putting away the sacramentals, my eyes wandered around the pitiful congregation. Since this chapel was part of a Catholic medical center, it was shared primarily by the geriatric wing and the psychiatric wing for those patients who were well enough to attend or, in some cases, had permission from their psychiatrists to attend. Wheelchairs were everywhere, and the few patients who were ambulatory were quite aged and crippled from their years. It was depressing. I found it difficult to see how this scene could lift anyone from a depression until my friend nudged me and whispered, "Look around, Father Ken. What do you see?"

The old faces stared blankly toward the altar. The patients in wheelchairs were all wrapped up in crocheted and knitted afghans, and some of the people held rosaries in their wrinkled hands. For the most part, I felt their faces were expressionless, almost submissive to the effects of time.

"Look closely, Father Ken . . . except for the clothes, it's difficult to tell the little old men from the little old women."

I studied the faces more closely. "My God, you're right." I had never made this observation before that moment, but it was true. Many of the women's hair were kept short . . . for hygienic reasons probably . . .

and age seemed to soften the men's features. I looked on in amazement.

"It's strange, isn't it, Father Ken? If we were to visit the nursery and the newborns at the general hospital, we couldn't pick out the boy babies from the girl babies. They're all dressed alike."

I agreed with her. She interrupted my thoughts with, "It's the life cycle, Father. We're born into this world helpless, and many of us leave it helpless . . . what counts is the time we have in between when we can choose for ourselves. Somehow, all the things that we feel are important to us now, and all the things we may strive to acquire during our lives, gradually become insignificant when we look toward Eternity."

Later, we sat in the parlor and she shared with me what led up to her turning back to God. "I was so miserable, and the pain I felt inside seemed to consume me more every day. Shutting God out because of my hurt and anger didn't relieve my suffering . . . if anything, it became worse. Where do you go with grief, and how can you make sense of it or make sense of anything? God didn't turn away from me just because I wanted to shut

Him out. The only reason I went to the chapel that first afternoon was because I was out of cigarettes, and since I could not go anywhere unescorted, I told the nurse I would attend Mass with the small group she was taking to the chapel. I knew we would have to pass the canteen and I could purchase a pack of cigarettes. I was desperate to smoke and even if it meant that I would have to put in that time at Mass, it would be worth it. I was determined not to participate, genuflect, or anything else . . . just put in the thirty minutes, then go back to the ward and light up. But when I got in the chapel and looked around me, I couldn't take my eyes away from the people gathered here. Suddenly, it was as if something clicked inside. My mind began to race with a thousand thoughts until finally I just looked up at the altar and sat there. In the silence, I felt that God had something to tell me. You see, Father Ken, I was bitter because I had prayed and trusted God to do MY will, but I never really prayed to accept His will."

She admitted that she still felt the pain of her family and marriage being broken, but she was confident that she would have the strength to cope with this suffering, knowing that it was all a part of God's plan. And although she didn't understand it, she would accept it and *trust* God to see her through it all.

God spoke to her in that hospital chapel through the people around her, and in the silence she heard Him point out the need to look beyond her sufferings and pain and direct her vision toward eternal life.

With her consent, I shared her story with you in an effort to persuade you to look deeper into your own prayer life and perhaps better understand the need to pray for the virtue of acceptance. It is the sure way to find peace in the midst of trials.

All of us, you and I, must be aware of how very important our prayer life is and how very necessary it is to acquire the practice of "turning ourselves over to God." We NEED God and we NEED to communicate with Him so we can be prepared to accept the sorrows, as well as the joys, that life holds for us. Life is always a combination of both, happy and sad, good days and bad, but how you deal with it is very much determined by your trust in God and faith in His plan for you. Keeping the communication open between you and Our Lord is vital to your spirit of acceptance.

When you pray, don't keep pestering God to do YOUR will; pray for the grace to accept His . . . then TRUST Him. It is true about God . . . FATHER DOES KNOW BEST!

PRACTICAL APPLICATIONS

1. Looking back over your life, have you ever turned away from God because you were bitter and didn't understand the suffering that came to you?

2. Was the pain any easier to bear without Him?

3. When you pray, do you always ask God to do what you want Him to do?

4. In the past, when you finally accepted the cross God sent you, did you feel strength?

5. Are you often afraid that if you surrender your will to God, He will ask more of you than you are willing to give?

PRAY IT AGAIN, SAM

'Here I Am, Lord, . . . Do Something!'

In the last chapter you read about a woman who had always been close to God, but who turned away from Him when she faced what she thought was unbearable suffering. She is not alone. I have met many people who claim to have a personal relationship with God when things are "comfortable," when they feel they are in control . . . but let things go badly and it's "blame-God time." Then there are others who hang in there with God through good times and bad, accepting His will throughout it all. These are the people who have peace.

I do a great deal of work with organizations for the handicapped and shut-ins, and almost unanimously I have found these groups of people to project a peace I seldom find in the healthy, active people I meet in my retreat and mission ministry. It always amazes me how joyful they are, and you need only to look at them to feel their physical suffering and limitations.

Many times when I address these groups, I refer to them as "God's favorites." And I am one hundred percent sincere when I say that they make Christ more real to me through their beautiful witness. I tell them often how very special they are because God has singled them out. He knows they can take it. They have attached meaning to their sufferings and pain by offering themselves as witnesses to the suffering Christ in the world today. What a special vocation! They have been called to "suffer for Christ" in a visible way through their physical illness and handicaps.

But what about the people who also suffer, but in a way the world cannot immediately recognize? Perhaps you are one of them. Perhaps you know the suffering of loneliness, the suffering of being separated from a loved one, the suffering of being misjudged, the suffering of feeling unloved, the suffering of widowhood, the suffering of divorce, the suffering of caring for a sick relative or friend, the suffering of losing a child, the suffering of emotional illness, the suffering of anxiety or depression.

Each suffering is different, but what all suffering has in common is the pain. What do we do with the pain? How we react to it depends greatly on what kind of relationship we have with Our Lord.

There seems to be a modern spirituality that claims that all pain and suffering are evil . . . if we really "know the Lord," we won't have pain; if our faith is strong enough, we will be free from all ills that befall us. With that type of thinking, God becomes a cure-all, an analgesic that wipes away all pain and suffering. Not true. Jesus knew God, but He had His agony in the garden. Remember the Scripture, "Father, if it be thy will, let this cup pass from me" (Mt 26:39). Don't be misled by thinking that once you have committed your life to Our Lord, you will be free of suffering and pain. Don't play "Parker Brothers Jesus" by making a game of your Christ-commitment. "Okay, Lord, I'll turn my life over to you if you do this for me." (I'll give you Boardwalk if you give me Park Place.) Roll your prayers twice, pass pain, and go straight to joy!

There's nothing wrong in asking God for consolation during trial. Jesus asked for the "cup" to pass from Him. But for some people, the only time the Lord hears from them is when they're in a jam. I am merely trying to convince you of the need for a personal relationship with God, one in which you share everything with Him, the good and the bad; then when things get tough, letting God take control of your life and your strife will not be such an awesome task.

I'm sure you've heard the expression "the patience of Job." I think "trust" would have been a better word to describe his virtue. By the world's standards, Job had the best of everything, good family, health, wealth, success, but first and foremost, he was God's faithful servant. The devil claimed that Job wouldn't be so true-blue to God if adversity came his way, so poor Job was put to the test.

Everything went wrong, and Job got the worst of everything. For a time, Job was really angry with God (he must have been pretty close to the Lord to get by with telling God off like he did), yet he persevered through all the hardship and misery that came his way. Although he voiced his feelings about all the grief in his life, he still trusted that God would carry him through the bad times. Job certainly had a vision of eternal life. His faith did not go unrewarded. "And the Lord restored the fortune of Job" (Job 42:10).

The lesson to be learned is quite clear. Job could not have endured all that pain and suffering if he had not believed totally that God was with him.

And so it is with us. I can't stress enough the *need* to incorporate in our daily lives the habit of prayer — that "lifting up of our minds and hearts to God," that communication with our Heavenly Father.

Being human, all of us may question God at times. Job did, but that's where faith comes in, for even though we question, we still say, "Here I am, Lord . . . I don't know what You have in mind but I'll turn everything over to You." Then, to say, "Do something!" is, in fact, a statement of trust. We're saying, "I can't do it without You, God, so I trust You to run the show. Take over my life."

Looking back over my own life, I can see how at times I was angry with God when things didn't go as planned, but honestly, in retrospect, I must admit that I put myself in the driver's seat. I invited God to go where I took Him; I wasn't willing to go where He was leading me. I thought I knew what was best for me. I pursued what *I* wanted, but God had something else in mind. Each time when I was backed against the wall, I felt frustrated and defeated, until finally I had to get on my knees and pray.

I'm not certain to whom I can credit this statement, but I do know that the RECOVERY INCORPORATED organization, a support group for nervous patients, uses it: "Work like everything depends on you and pray like everything depends on God."

What a powerful piece of advice. You are taking the responsibility for your life trusting God to guide you, but you won't know where He is leading you unless you keep the lines of communication open with Him. The Lord's line is always open waiting to hear from us . . . it's our line that is giving the "busy" signal as we pursue what WE want without "calling home" to see if it's what our Heavenly Father wants.

I remember a retreatant, a very joyful woman, who shared her feelings about God: "He's so available!" And it's true. You don't need an appointment, a special place, or a special time for God. You need only to call out His name . . . then, just as the song says, "You got a friend." Just say, "Here I am, Lord, do something." He will.

PRACTICAL APPLICATIONS

1. Do you have a tendency to forget about God when things are going well and you feel you are in control?

2. When you are faced with decisions, do you ask God to guide you?

3. Is there a suffering in your life that you hang on to rather than letting God handle it for you? Perhaps it's bitterness because you feel that you have been wronged, or a feeling of hurt because you have been misunderstood. Maybe there is someone you feel angry about, and you permit this feeling to rob you of peace. Think about it.

PRAY IT AGAIN, SAM

PART THREE

Different Ways to Pray

6

You and Me, Lord

THERE ARE NO SUBSTITUTES FOR PRIVATE PRAYER. One retreat master compared it to a well-known soft-drink slogan, "It's the pause that refreshes." Even in the Gospels, we read about the numerous times Jesus went off by Himself to pray alone. Jesus needed His Father's guidance. He needed that communication to know His will. If Jesus Christ, the perfect person, needed to pray . . .what about us?

A child once asked me, "Father, how come Jesus needed to pray if He was God . . . who did He pray to, Himself?"

Well, Jesus was God, but He was also a man, a human person, as real as you and I. He showed us by His example that He, the perfect person, needed to pray alone. Shouldn't we have the same need? Remember, we aren't perfect.

How can you know God or yourself unless you spend time alone in His presence where He will speak to you in your heart?

You will discover secrets and insights of which you have never dreamed. But you have to do your share . . . you must "put" yourself in the presence of God.

Look at your prayer life thus far in your life. *How* do you pray? Do you do all the talking, telling God things He already knows?

Psalm 139 reads:

"O Lord, you have probed me and you know me; you know when I sit and when I stand.

"You understand my thoughts from afar."

Later in the chapter, Psalm 139 goes on to say:

"You have formed my inmost being; you knit me in my mother's womb." That Scripture passage seems quite clear . . . God knew you even before you were aware of yourself, even before you existed. There's no doubt, God knows you well, but how well do you know Him?

After Samuel realized that God was calling out to Him, he answered, "Speak, Lord, your servant is listening!" When you pray, do you say, "Listen, Lord, your servant is speaking"? Do you program God to do your will?

"Make me well. Sell my house. Give us rain. Give us sunshine. Make me have peace. Get me out of this jam. Don't let me suffer. LISTEN, LORD, YOUR SERVANT IS SPEAKING!"

God knows what you need (though often it isn't what YOU think you need) before you even ask Him. All of us have learned the art of praying FOR something, but not all of us have learned how to be in His presence. Not all of us have learned to listen.

One of the simplest prayer exercises and definitely the easiest to learn is "the prayer of centering," and it stems back to the early Church and the time of St. Benedict. It's an excellent way of putting yourself in God's Presence . . . better still, making you aware of His presence.

Read the following instructions carefully: Sit back in a comfortable position. Keep your head erect, then close your eyes. Rest your hands on your knees. Just relax for a few seconds. Now let go of your thoughts and anxieties. Become aware of your breathing . . . don't hurry it or slow it down.

As you breathe out, let the word "Jesus" come from deep inside you. When thoughts and images pass before your mind, let them flow like a stream of water over rocks.

Concentrate only on the word "Jesus." When other sounds pierce your ears, shut them out and tune in only "Jesus." Do this for a few moments. Keep repeating "Jesus" in rhythm with your breathing. Now, put the book down and try it. Then be still and listen. . . .

* * * * * * *

Assuming you have followed my instructions, you should feel quite relaxed right now. Isn't this a beautiful prayer? And it's so very, very simple. With daily practice, you'll find it will require less and less time to reach that state of concentration, that state of awareness of God's presence and peace.

The prayer of centering can be a total prayer or a "warm-up" prayer, depending on what prayer practice you wish to cultivate. If you are accustomed to reading Scripture meditations, use this prayer before you begin, to clear your mind and predispose yourself to deeper concentration.

I personally recommend this prayer exercise for everyone, but especially those who have pressured, busy days. You don't need a prayer book or a Bible to use it, and you can be anywhere, at any time. This prayer comes from inside of you. You will be surprised how addictive it is. Once you have felt God's peace run through you, you will want to experience it more often . . . this intimate union with Our Lord. And this is the stuff saints are made of!

Here's an interesting observation I would like to share with you:

Do you remember way back when (if you were brought up in Catholic schools) . . . the teacher, usually a nun, would ask this question from the old Baltimore Catechism, "Why did God make you?"

If you studied your homework, you would answer what you had memorized, "God made me to know Him, to love Him, and to serve Him, in this world and be happy with Him in heaven." Can't you just hear those singsong little voices?

As children, that's what we memorized, but later in life, especially when we tried to make sense of it all — what life is all about — we might have asked ourselves that same question.

"Why *did* God make me?" The answer is

still the same, "To KNOW Him, to LOVE Him, to SERVE Him."

When we veer away from why God made us is when we get into trouble and we lose peace. Keep this in mind. We can't love someone we don't know, any more than we want to serve someone we don't know. So . . . get to KNOW God better. You may have read volumes of theology books and maybe you can quote Scripture right and left; you may know all ABOUT God, but do you KNOW God? One thing is certain, you're not going to know Him unless you spend time alone with Him in private prayer.

I find, and others have agreed, that practicing the prayer of centering daily brings a new awareness of God's presence in our lives throughout each day, even those times when we are not at prayer. We gradually become more alert to Him working in us and we "hear" Him speaking to us in our thoughts and in others with whom we work.

I promise you, once you acquire the habit of being alone with Christ, not only will you know Him better, you will love Him more, and you will want to serve Him. Even at your busiest times, when your mind is racing with a thousand thoughts and pressures mount, you will feel His presence and you will be aware of an inner strength as a little voice deep within reminds you, "You and me, Lord."

PRACTICAL APPLICATIONS

1. Do you spend most of your prayer time asking God for favors?

2. Have you ever just sat quietly and thought about His plan for you?

3. During times of stress, have you ever felt His presence giving you the courage to carry on?

4. Do you really believe that you have developed a personal relationship with Our Lord?

5. Do you better realize the need for private prayer to develop this relationship?

PRAY IT AGAIN, SAM

7

Bring Out the Beads

If you've attended any parish missions or retreats that I have directed, you are aware by now that I definitely feel Our Blessed Mother has a role in our prayer life. People never hesitate to ask a priest or minister to pray for them, so why can't we ask the same favor of the Mother of Jesus? Besides, who has more "pull" than she has with Christ? Remember the wine at Cana?

I am also very much in favor of *praying* the rosary. Somehow, after the Vatican II Council, a misunderstanding arose about devotion to Our Lady . . . but I challenge anyone to show me where, in the Vatican II writings, it directs us to eliminate Mary and the rosary. Unfortunately, for a time it became unpopular to conduct any Marian devotions or to preach about Mary, and that's too bad. Mary, as the mother of Jesus, played a precise role in our redemption. Also, she completes the family of the Church — with God, our Father, Jesus, our Brother, and

Mary, our Mother. This is scripturally sound. Read John 19:27: "There is your mother." Jesus shares His mother with us just as He did with the "disciple whom he loved," John. For those of you who feel that the rosary is "old-fashioned," let me point out that as a meditative tool, the rosary is no more old-fashioned than Scripture, since each of the fifteen mysteries of the rosary is taken from the Bible.

THE FIVE JOYFUL MYSTERIES:

1. The Annunciation — Luke 1:26-38.
2. The Visitation — Luke 1:39-56.
3. The Nativity — Luke 2:1-20.
4. The Presentation — Luke 2:22-39.
5. Finding in the Temple — Luke 2:41-51.

THE FIVE SORROWFUL MYSTERIES:

1. Agony in the Garden — Mark 14:32-42.
2. Scourging at the Pillar — Mark 15:15.
3. Crowning with Thorns — Mark 15:16-20.
4. Carrying of the Cross — John 19:17.
5. The Crucifixion — Luke 23:33-49.

THE FIVE GLORIOUS MYSTERIES:

1. The Resurrection — Mark 16:1-8.

2. The Ascension — Mark 16:19.
3. The Descent of the Holy Spirit — Acts 2, 4.
4. Assumption of the Blessed Virgin Mary — Revelation 12.
5. Crowning of the Blessed Virgin Mary — Revelation 12.

Today, there are many books available depicting the scriptural rosary, with meditations from the Bible which makes each mystery more alive to you.

My mother had a beautiful approach to the rosary. She carried it in her apron pocket during the day and it was almost always on her person. Many a time, I would come in and find her alone at the kitchen table, with her eyes closed and her lips moving silently as her fingers moved from one bead to another. I can still hear her: "Hello, Kenny, I'm waiting for the kettle to boil."

She had learned the art of "wasting time with God" by not wasting a few minutes here or there throughout her day, but rather she would use those precious moments to be in His presence, through her rosary.

She used "worry beads" before it was considered psychologically therapeutic. It is amusing that therapists recognize the value in the "worry stone," a smooth rock to rub between your thumb and fingers. It's supposed to help release the locked-up anxiety, worry, and tension by projecting it all to the stone (sort of rubbing it out of you onto the stone).

There are beads available to do the same thing. It's simply a string of beads that are fingered to release inner anxieties. If we look at the rosary from a psychological standpoint alone, it has merit, but when you combine that with faith, it's powerful.

I gave this account in my autobiography, PLAYBOY TO PRIEST, but I feel that it bears repeating now.

The night before I was to leave for the seminary I missed seeing my brother Roy and his son, my godchild, Christopher, who was barely a year old. They came by the house to wish me well, but they had to leave before I returned home.

When I entered the house, I found my mother and her brother, Uncle John, before the television. The newsman was narrating an account of a fatal automobile accident that had occurred just a few blocks from our home. The names of the victims were being withheld until the family could be notified.

When I inquired about what was happening, my mother "hushed" me with a gesture to be still. "Some poor mother's son has just been killed," she whispered, then reached for her beads in her apron pocket. When she closed her eyes and began to pray, I felt a sinking feeling in the pit of my stomach, but I wasn't certain why. Shortly after that, our parish priest, Father Walshe, came to our door to give Mom the news that Roy and Christopher had both been killed.

My reaction was violent . . . I was angry at God. Roy and Christopher didn't deserve to die, and my mother certainly didn't deserve the grief their deaths would bring. I thrashed about the parlor, cursing.

I was angry, sad, bitter . . . everything. That was my reaction, but my mother's was just the opposite. She consoled me and tried to make me understand that we must be willing to surrender to God's will. She used the sorrow of the Blessed Mother as an example of complete submission. "Her son was killed too."

She was unbelievable as she accepted this

cross that God sent her and drew upon the example of Our Lady to give her strength. She didn't question God's will; she surrendered to it as she knelt down and began to pray. What a tremendous relationship my mother had with her Lord and what grace she must have received through her rosary devotion to prepare her for the suffering she was experiencing.

I must tell you how grateful I have always been for my mother's childlike simplicity and faith. Even now, though she's been dead for more than twenty years, her words keep coming back to me. What patience and perseverance she displayed and how very wise she was!

I recall how I would return from Rome each summer while I was in the seminary, eager to share all the profound things I had learned. That last summer before I was ordained, I was all pumped up. I would be one of the "new breed" of post-Vatican II priests. I had read, studied, listened to lectures, and was on top of all that was happening. After I spent that first evening trying to impress Mother with all my knowledge and my insight into prayer, she merely said, as if she were attempting to pacify me, "That's nice, Kenny."

I thought, "My God . . . is that all she can say? 'That's nice, Kenny'?" Here I was practically an authority, ready to teach her how to develop her spiritual life from all that I had learned about prayer and faith in my head, but it was all what she already knew in her heart.

When I explained to her that experts at meditation advise repeating a word or phrase over and over (the use of a mantra) and chanting, because both free our conscious mind and block out distractions so that we may be lifted up to a higher state, she said, "Like we do in the rosary, Kenny?"

"I wasn't referring to the rosary, Mother," I answered, somewhat discouraged. I had something more sophisticated in mind.

"But Kenny, why can't we do that with the Hail Mary? It's such a beautiful prayer."

I didn't agree with her then, but I will admit now that she was right. "Why can't we do that with the rosary and the 'Hail Mary'? . . . and it is a beautiful prayer." Think about the words:

"Hail Mary, full of grace, the Lord is

with you. Blessed are you among women and blessed is the fruit of your womb, Jesus. [We have just acknowledged, from Scripture, the importance of Mary's role as Mother of God.]

"Holy Mary, Mother of God, pray for us sinners now and at the hour of our death."

(Here we are asking her to pray FOR us and to be with us when we prepare to meet her Son, to share eternal life with Him.)

God knows my mother always kept that vision of eternal life in her simplicity and faith. Her rosary was her worry beads, her meditation, her mantra, and when she died, they found her beside her bed with her rosary clasped between her fingers. It was also her consolation.

"Holy Mary, mother of God, pray for us sinners now and at the hour of our death. Amen."

PRACTICAL APPLICATIONS

1. When is the last time you PRAYED the rosary?

2. Have you ever really meditated on the

mysteries and tried to create that scene in your mind?

3. Can you recall if you have ever reached for a rosary to give you consolation in times of grief and tribulation?

4. Have you ever felt a need to ask for prayers?

Why not ask Mary?

PRAY IT AGAIN, SAM

8

Feelings, Nothing More (or Less) Than Feelings

A great emphasis is put on feelings today, but there's a good deal of misunderstanding about them too, especially regarding prayer. Although it is true that feelings play an important role in our spiritual life, it is fruitless to base our closeness to Our Lord on how we "feel" when we pray.

All of us have experienced some emotional moments during prayer or while attending a prayer service. For instance, something that almost always moves me is hearing "Silent Night" sung on Christmas Eve. I'm sure this is partly due to the memories I have of my childhood, when my mother would light the plum pudding while our whole family gathered around the table to sing this familiar carol. These were happy times in my past, so when the memories come flooding in, I feel a certain swelling in my chest . . . but there's some sadness there too, since I am separated from my loved ones by either distance or death.

You may have a certain hymn or prayer that stirs emotion within you too, but generally speaking, we don't always feel something when we pray. If you do, that's good, but if you don't feel anything, don't worry about it. Even the mystics (the prayer experts) experience dry spells in their spiritual life, but that doesn't mean that their prayers, or yours and mine, are less pleasing to God. In fact, there would be little merit if we were always "high" on Our Lord.

It's amusing to hear some folk refer to various forms of prayer by using the expression "It doesn't *DO* anything for me." What they are really saying is that they don't "feel" anything. Granted, different ways of praying are appealing to different people, but no prayer goes without reward. Just because you don't feel it doesn't mean Our Lord isn't listening. And if you do feel it, be grateful . . . it's sort of a bonus from God for your efforts.

As you grow in your spiritual life, you

probably will experience the difference between meditation and contemplation. In simple language, meditation employs our thoughts. Contemplation employs our feelings. You might compare it to the difference between looking at a glass of water to tasting it.

In contemplation your senses come into action, and a more intense concentration is required. Now, not everyone can contemplate ALL of the time . . . not even those who are called to a life of contemplative prayer.

Maybe this hypothetical situation will give you a better understanding of feelings and their importance, and lack of importance, in our spiritual life. You may be able to gain a clearer perspective.

You promise you are going to spend one half hour in private prayer every day, and let's suppose you choose a quiet, empty church. You kneel and begin your prayer. Nothing comes to you — you're dried up — so you reach for your Bible and begin to read, but your mind keeps wandering. "I have to stop at the grocery on the way home . . . I hope the cleaners have my suit ready . . . I feel like I'm gaining weight . . . I should lose about ten pounds." Bothered by these distractions, you close your eyes and ask God to lift these thoughts from you so you can really pray. You look at your watch. *Only five minutes* have gone by, and it seemed more like twenty! You start all over, but throughout the remaining twenty-five minutes, you keep looking at your watch. The time drags. Finally, your half hour has passed. You have read Scripture; you've talked things over with the Lord; you even prayed your rosary. As you genuflect, you feel satisfied that you put in your thirty minutes, but you're not certain how effective your prayer time was.

The next day, you go back and do it again. One line of Scripture jumps out at you, and your mind and heart begin to race. While just looking at the crucifix you feel you are "lifted up to the Lord." Nothing is important to you . . . only this intense communion with Jesus. Suddenly you hear the church bells ring and you realize the time. You look at your watch, but you can't believe the thirty minutes have passed so quickly because you feel as though you just got there. You really hate to leave this place and don't want to part with the secure peace and joy that you have just experienced.

Okay, take a good look at these two situations which I have described. If I were to ask you which day you felt you got the most from that thirty minutes, you wouldn't hesitate to answer, "The second day." That's because your prayer came easy to you and you "felt" something, but that doesn't mean that the first day was a waste. Not at all. You see, the first day, you did God the favor; the second day, He did a favor for you.

Feeling something in prayer is God's gift to you. When you pray and feel nothing, that's your gift to God. So don't be discouraged. Incidentally, the prayer of centering does help on days when distractions keep haunting you, but know that you're going to have these kinds of days when prayer is difficult. That's when God is asking you to do all the work. Persevere; it's worth it.

A mother of five small children once told me how difficult it was for her to "keep holy thoughts" in her mind when she prayed. She said she was always distracted by her preoccupation with her children and the duties that required her attention. Then finally, one day, she said, "Look God, you gave me all this responsibility and I'm doing the best job I can . . . if you want me to 'think holy,' then put the thoughts there."

Soon, she said, at her busiest times, she "felt" God's constant presence. She compared it to a fatherly hug, and the awareness was so strong that she would feel compelled to respond by saying, "I love you, Lord."

You see, God blessed her by permitting her to feel something, and her approach was really very honest. She offered Him all her efforts, even her distractions.

You can do the same . . . tell Him how you feel when you don't "feel" like praying. He already knows, but tell Him anyway. Share your day with God, not just that "alone" time.

That same mother also shared this with me. After she was tired and sometimes feeling as if her job was a thankless one, she would steal a few minutes away from her routine and rest awhile with Jesus. "Father, I imagine Jesus just sitting there watching me as I go about my tasks, then in my mind, I see Him motion for me to come and sit beside Him. Often I rest my head on His knee and He pats my shoulder. I know He understands me . . . and He loves me. Then, I return to my chores refreshed because I know I'm doing what He wants me to do . . . and He's always there right beside me."

She certainly developed a personal relationship with Our Lord, and you can do the same, if you haven't already.

Christ is so available, so flexible, so ready to be anywhere you want Him to be, so ready to reach out and "pat your shoulder," so ready to give you consolation, so ready to fill you with His strength, and so ready to flood you with His love.

So, if you don't feel like praying, tell Him so, then pray anyway. He knows you and He loves you the way you are, but you'll never "feel" His love unless you make yourself available to Him. He's always available to you!

PRACTICAL APPLICATIONS

1. Do you know the difference between thoughts and feelings?

2. Do you become discouraged when you don't feel anything at prayer?

3. Have you ever offered up your distractions to God as well as your good works?

4. Is there any certain prayer or hymn that taps your emotions? Do you know why?

5. Do you give up too easily when prayer doesn't come easily to you?

PRAY IT AGAIN, SAM

9

Signs or Coincidence

Signs are all around us. You can't go through a day without seeing them, even when you don't realize it. When you pass a store, a sign tells you the name of the shop. On each corner, you will see a sign telling you the name of the street. When you go to work, a sign will tell you the name of your company. Even if you watch television, there will be a sign of what channel to choose and a sign will appear on the screen to identify the name of the program. These are all signs you can see. There are also signs you can hear: your alarm clock buzzing in the morning, telling you it's time to start your day; church bells, chiming the Angelus; the telephone ringing to alert you that someone is trying to contact you, and the doorbell announcing someone has come to call.

Whether audible, or visible, all are signs because they indicate a fact or direction.

Think of it, our daily lives are governed by signs telling us what we're to do and when, and we refer to them constantly. How often do you look at your watch or a clock?

So it's established . . . you all recognize that there are signs all around you, but what about those signs you can't see or hear? What about supernatural signs that you can't easily recognize or explain, the signs that God gives you?

Pertaining to spirituality, I like this definition: "A sign is a coincidence . . . plus faith." Often God's signs can be difficult to determine, but occasionally the Lord does everything short of an apparition or a knock on the head to let you know His direction.

I can attest to this fact in my own life and the paths that led me to the priesthood. If you have read my autobiography, you know how I lived a fast life for a time as a steward with a British airline, and I must admit I loved the glitter of travel, money, and association with affluent people. The first sign I had pointing me to the seminary I didn't recognize, but in retrospect I see it was there and it came from a nun, one of Mother Teresa's sisters in Calcutta. She counseled me about saving my soul and warned me about my misplaced priorities. She went even further by suggesting that I could have a vocation. That was absurd as far as I was concerned because I was engaged to be married within a year and I had a job I loved. No way was I going to give all that up to be a priest! But in less than a year, my fiancée broke our engagement and I lost my job with the airline. Signs? Perhaps, but it seems more than coincidence that the two biggest obstacles in the path for the priesthood were removed and both were beyond my control.

I still wasn't looking toward the religious life. In fact, I was lucky if I even got to Mass on Sundays. The world still held too many "good times" for me, so I took a job as an interpreter on the ocean liner *Queen Elizabeth* and continued to indulge myself with travel, glitter, and affluent people. But it was while I was working aboard ship that I began to attend Mass more regularly, and that was only because they needed someone who knew how to serve Mass for the Catholic chaplain. Since I was Catholic and I admitted remembering the fundamentals of serving Mass, I was recruited. Another sign?

The idea of the priesthood would stab my consciousness once in a while, but I fought like hell to reject it. I did pray more, because I didn't feel peace and I wasn't certain why I didn't, since I was trying to live a more sober life and I didn't indulge myself as much as I had done while with the airlines. There was always an uneasiness, a discontented feeling stirring inside me.

Then, one day after Mass the priest approached me and out of the clear blue asked, "Son, have you ever thought you might have a vocation?" It really shook me. Why would he ask me that? He ended the conversation with, "I'm going to pray that God sends you a sign to show you His will." I had mixed emotions over his offer, because even if I did get the sign he was talking about, I wasn't sure that I wanted to be a priest.

Within a few months, a bishop was aboard the liner, and he and I began to chat after Mass. He asked me a lot about myself and my background, and before I knew it I found myself pouring out my whole past to him. He told me he believed that God was calling me to the priesthood, and if I was willing to give some serious thought and prayer to the prospect, he would grant me admittance to his diocesan seminary.

That did it. After the ship docked and I was driving home, I said, "Okay, Lord, if this is what you want — and you obviously do — I'll apply for the seminary." At that moment of decision, I felt a flood of peace beyond all description. That was my sign, the peace I experienced when I surrendered to God's will. Suddenly, I WANTED to be a priest; the very thing that I had fought became something I wanted. So, here I am today, an ex-playboy sharing with you the joys that await you when you let God take over your life and communicate with Him daily in private prayer. Believe me, to grow in the knowledge of Jesus Christ and to serve Him is the most exciting experience you will ever have. It certainly has been that for me.

You may have had a similar experience in your own life, a set of circumstances, or sometimes people, guiding you along in a certain direction, but you didn't know what was at the end of the line until you got there. Finally, when you arrived at that place in time where God wanted you to be, you had peace.

Really, that is the one definite sign we can always recognize, the peace that God gives us when we are doing His will, when we make the decision to follow where He is leading us. If you make a major decision in your life and you still do not have peace, pray hard and look again. Examine whether you are pursuing your will or His.

You know, regardless of how many signs the Lord sends you, you're not going to recognize them and respond to them if you're not opening up for Him to work in your life. As I described before, a sign is a coincidence, plus faith, so have faith in Him to control your life. I promise He'll do a better job than you do.

Occasionally, people come to me and say, "I don't know what to do, Father. I keep looking for a sign." I often wonder if they are not asking God to do all the work. Sometimes you must proceed with faith. You have to prove yourself to God . . . don't ask Him to prove Himself to you. Search out what He wants for you, then pray.

Do you notice how we always arrive

back at that same thing, prayer? There's just no substitute for it, no other way to put God in your life, no other way to know His will, no other way to keep the vision of eternal life.

Just as I described the word "sign" earlier as something to indicate a fact or direction, a sign is also a symbol, an identifying feature, or a distinctive mark. When we make the Sign of the Cross, we distinguish ourselves as Catholic Christians, but are you aware of just what that sign means? It's more than just a preface to prayer, or God's call letters. Be aware that each time you make the Sign of the Cross, you are acknowledging that Jesus Christ died on the cross so we could gain eternal life; and you are professing your belief in the Holy Trinity, that there is one God, but three persons, the Father, the Son and the Holy Spirit.

A lot of credit must go to the Holy Spirit, "who dwells among us." It is no coincidence that you are reading this book; rather, it's a sign that you want to grow in your spirituality. Perhaps you have learned something that you can incorporate into your prayer life that will enable you to achieve that goal.

Whether you realize it or not, you too are a sign. It's important for you to examine in what direction you may be leading others. As you deepen your Christ-commitment, know that He will use you to draw others to Him. It's bound to happen, because as you experience His love more fully, it will show. That love will pour out and touch the people around you. You are a sign *for* Christ, a witness to His peace that can only be found in knowing, loving, and serving Him.

"And they'll know we are Christians by our love."

PART FOUR

How to Meditate

10

'Imagine That!'

Imagination. What is it? If you're human and you can "think," then you can imagine. It seems that some people confuse imagination with creativity, but there is a difference. Have you ever heard "I just don't have any imagination"? What is really meant is, "I just don't have the creativity." If you can think, you can imagine. We all daydream, don't we? So what do we do when we daydream? We project in our minds a different place, a different time, but most often, we are in the scene.

For those of you who still argue that you have no imagination, here's a test:

Think about this scene in your mind and put yourself "in the picture" as you read these words:

See yourself in your kitchen. Walk to your refrigerator.

See the light go on as you open the door.

Let your eyes skim over the contents.

See the milk, the cheese, the eggs, the leftovers.

Open the crisper.

Feel the cold touch as you pull the drawer.

Take out a lemon.

Close the refrigerator door.

The light is gone.

Look at the yellow color of the lemon.

Feel the rough rind as you rub your fingers across it.

Still holding the lemon, open the cutlery drawer.

Take out a sharp knife.

Place the lemon on a cutting board.

Cut it in half.

Look at the few drops of juice that run from the fruit.

Now, put the half of lemon to your mouth and suck out some of the juice.

Can you taste it? Is it sour? I have had retreatants tell me that they have experienced salivation when they imagined that sour taste. Whether you have salivated or not, if you concentrated on my directions, you did "get the picture" in your mind. And that is what imagination is, creating pictures, places, things, and people in your mind.

You may not have realized it before, but imagination plays a vital part in your prayer life if you are to develop meditation.

Meditation is sometimes referred to as "active prayer" . . . we put ourselves in the picture and become a part of the scene.

A good formula for meditation when using Scripture is: READ, THINK, APPLY.

Let's meditate on the sixth station of the cross, Veronica wipes the face of Jesus. Just as with the lemon test, create the scene I describe in your mind, but this time put yourself in Veronica's place. See Jesus in the distance carrying His cross. Look at the crowd lined up in His path; some are mocking Him while others seem sad. Feel the heat of the sun bearing down on your shoulders.

Now, look at Christ's shoulders.

They are torn and lacerated from the rough wood of the cross.

Look at His face . . . His expression shows pain.

His face is wet with perspiration and

blood dripping from the crown of thorns embedded in His temples.

He limps closer to you.

You can see His pain.

What can you do?

Suddenly He falls under the weight of the cross.

A soldier cracks a whip demanding Him to get on His feet.

Can you hear the whip slash at His flesh?

You want to help Him.

You're holding a cloth in your hands.

Should you wipe the blood and sweat from His face?

Will the soldiers punish you if you interfere?

What will the onlookers think? What will they do?

You press the cloth against His face. Can you feel the warm moisture of His sweat and blood?

As you withdraw the cloth, His eyes meet yours.

They are pained, sad . . . but they look right through you. You want to help Him more, to offer Him some consolation, but the soldiers push you back into the crowd.

How do you feel?

Do you feel helpless?

What else can you do?

Now try to fathom what you have just experienced. The Christ-man has suffered for you. How can you respond to this immense love? Apply this to your life.

How often have you felt that Jesus was calling you to a deeper union with Him?

What held you back?

Was it uncomfortable to come forth and be called a Christ-lover just as it was for Veronica, who pondered over the crowd's reaction?

If you had been in the crowd, some of them quite militant, would you have the courage to comfort the suffering Christ?

Put down this book and think about it for a few moments.

* * * * * * *

Congratulations! You have just made a meditation.

PRACTICAL APPLICATIONS

I have written a few meditations that will hopefully make you *think* and *apply*. Don't just read one and then go to the other; rather, read it, think about it, and then apply it to your personal circumstances. Pick out something, a line or word that jumps out at you, then put yourself in the presence of God, and LISTEN.

PRAY IT AGAIN, SAM

SHORT MEDITATIONS

Blest Are They Who Believe
(John 20:24-31)

"Peace be with you," Jesus says as He
shows them His hands and His side.
The disciples rejoice.
HE HAS RISEN!
But where is Thomas?
The disciples want to share their joy,
But when they tell him,
He doesn't believe.
"I will never believe unless
I can put my fingers into
The nail marks of His hands
And my hand into His side."
The disciples are gathered again;
Thomas is with them when
Suddenly Jesus appears.
"Peace be with you."
Jesus turns to Thomas,
"Take your fingers and examine my
hands;
Put your hand into my side.
Do not persist in your disbelief,
Believe."

Thomas shouts,
"My Lord and My God!"
"You became a believer because you saw Me;
Blest are they who have not seen
. . . and have believed."

* * *

At Mass, when the priest says,
"This is my Body, This is my Blood,"
Do you believe Jesus is there?
If suddenly He appeared as a man,
Would you be like Thomas, and shout,
"My Lord and My God!"
Must He show Himself to you?
Where is your faith?
"Blest are they who have not seen
. . . and have believed."

Who Touched Me?
(Mark 5:21-43)

People are pushing and shoving
As Jesus and His disciples
Make their way through the crowd.

WHO TOUCHED ME?
Peter asks,
"Lord, do you not see the crowd?
Are we not so tightly packed?"
Jesus' eyes scan the many faces,
Searching.
WHO TOUCHED ME?
Christ stands still, then turns.
The crowd stops.
His eyes rest on a woman.
"It was I."
Trembling, she falls to her knees
And tells of her illness and her cure
She received by merely
Touching His garment.
Christ takes her face into His hands.
He reads her soul.
He sees her faith.
YOU TOUCHED ME.
A different time, different people.
Your parish church, crowded for Mass.
Some are listening — some are not.
One is looking at his watch.
They fill the aisles
At Communion time.
Will He ask again,
WHO TOUCHED ME?

Will He turn and search the pews?
Will His eyes rest on you?
Will you humbly kneel and say,
"IT WAS I"
Who reached out
And felt Your power?
When at the Sign of Peace,
I touched my neighbor
And saw the hidden Christ
With faith,
"I TOUCHED YOU."

Walk on the Water
(Matthew 14:22-33)

The storm is violent
As the waves whip
The side of the boat.
It is night and the
Apostles are frightened.
If only Jesus were with them. . . .
A figure moves across the water.
"Is it a ghost?"
Their fear mounts.
Jesus comforts them,
"It is I, do not be afraid."

106

Peter cries out,
"Lord, if it is You,
Tell me to come to You
Across the water."
"Come," Jesus answers.
Peter moves across the water
Toward Jesus.
Suddenly the wind grows stronger
And Peter becomes frightened. He begins
      to sink.
"Lord, save me!"
Jesus stretches
His hand to catch him.
"How little faith you have!
Why do you falter?"

* * *

Life has many storms,
And sometimes we are frightened,
So we turn to God for
Guidance and strength.
But doubts make us falter.
We cry out,
"Help me, Lord!"
We know we can't do it alone.
And always His hand

Is outstretched
To draw us closer to Him.
Peter faltered when he
Saw himself instead of seeing
Christ.
Take your eyes
Off you
And look at Him.

Transfiguration
(Matthew 17:1-8)

The steep mountain is difficult to climb.
Jagged rocks hurt their sandaled feet.
Peter, James, and John
Have been climbing all day.
Now, they rest.
When Jesus first asked them to be with
     Him
They were flattered,
But now they are tired
And their legs and backs ache.
It would have been easier if
The Lord had permitted them
To stay with the others.
Why is the journey so difficult,

Even painful?
Where is Jesus taking them?
Suddenly a brilliant light
Radiates from Jesus,
A glare so fierce, it blinds.
Christ's face is as bright as the sun.
And His garment is glistening white.
Moses and Elijah are at His side.
The Apostles are in ecstasy.
They don't want to leave this holy place.
But Jesus tells them,
"You must return to the world below."
Following Christ isn't easy.
Sometimes, we feel that
Being a Christian costs too much.
But just when we feel
Our efforts are in vain
And we can't go any farther,
Jesus gives us strength to continue.
Once we have answered His call,
We can't turn back.
We know we must follow Him.
Only in Jesus,
Can we find peace.

EPILOGUE

It has been a joy for me to share this book with you. As I told you in the Introduction, I am not an authority on prayer, so I can only share with you my personal experience and some of the things people have shared with me.

This book is merely an explanation of various forms of prayer, but hopefully, you have found one that appeals to you. So many beautiful books, written by very holy people, can deepen your insight into the Christ-life within us. I recommend you investigate them.

We're all striving to share eternal life with our Heavenly Father. Let's pray for each other.

God bless you.

ABOUT THE AUTHOR. . . .

English-born Father Kenneth J. Roberts presently resides in St. Louis, Missouri, but his unique apostolate takes him all over the United States. He has appeared on hundreds of radio and television shows and has earned a reputation as one of the most powerful preachers in the Catholic Church today. His dynamic personality on the pulpit carries over to his writings as he constantly stresses the positive truths of our Catholic Faith and urges people to look to Christ and His Church for peace and fulfillment. Father Roberts's appeal is to all ages.

OTHER BOOKS BY THE AUTHOR:

PLAYBOY TO PRIEST
In his autobiography, Father Roberts tells of his unique road to the priesthood. Prior to ordination at age 35, Father was a part of the jet set, traveling through Europe and the Far and Middle East. His adventures even included entanglement with a gold-smuggling operation. This book is both entertaining and inspirational as he describes his journey to the priesthood.

MARY, THE PERFECT PRAYER PARTNER
This provokes a deeper understanding and esteem for Our Lady as we learn to pray to God

through Mary, revealed as a model for everyone. A special section on the rosary will help you pray to Mary with renewed vigor. Three methods for praying the rosary are explained, with the mysteries beautifully portrayed to help you meditate on the life of Christ.

YOU BETTER BELIEVE IT

This popular catechism offers answers to youth in their own language, about God, about the teachings of the Church, and about themselves. It has been heralded by parents and religious educators as well as young people themselves.